THIS BOOK BELONGS TO

BEER NAME	IBU
STYLE	ABV
BATCH #	SRM / EBC
BATCH SIZE	EFFICIENCY
DATE	OG / FG

INGREDIENTS

FERMENTATION

SAMPLE DATE	TEMPERATURE	GRAVITY

BREWING NOTES

TASTE

HOP NOTE	☆☆☆☆☆
YEAST NOTE	☆☆☆☆☆
AROMA	☆☆☆☆☆
FLAVOUR	☆☆☆☆☆

🍺 BEERNAME	🌿 IBU
🌾 STYLE	🍾 ABV
🍻 BATCH #	🍺 SRM / EBC
🏭 BATCH SIZE	💲 EFFICIENCY
📅 DATE	🫧 OG / FG

INGREDIENTS

....	....	....	....
....	....	....	....
....	....	....	....
....	....	....	....
....	....	....	....

FERMENTATION

🔍 SAMPLE DATE	🌡 TEMPERATURE	🫧 GRAVITY

BREWING NOTES

TASTE

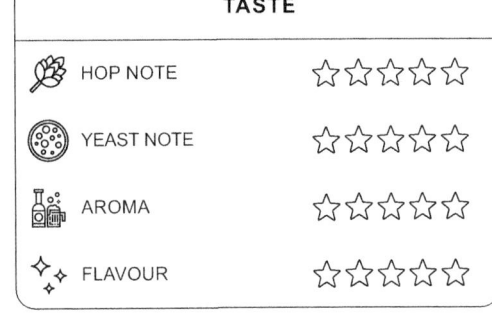

🌿 HOP NOTE	☆☆☆☆☆
🧫 YEAST NOTE	☆☆☆☆☆
🧪 AROMA	☆☆☆☆☆
✨ FLAVOUR	☆☆☆☆☆

BEERNAME	IBU
STYLE	ABV
BATCH #	SRM / EBC
BATCH SIZE	EFFICIENCY
DATE	OG / FG

INGREDIENTS

....	....	....	....
....	....	....	....
....	....	....	....
....	....	....	....
....	....	....	....

FERMENTATION

SAMPLE DATE	TEMPERATURE	GRAVITY

BREWING NOTES

TASTE

HOP NOTE	☆☆☆☆☆
YEAST NOTE	☆☆☆☆☆
AROMA	☆☆☆☆☆
FLAVOUR	☆☆☆☆☆

BEERNAME	
STYLE	
BATCH #	
BATCH SIZE	
DATE	

IBU	
ABV	
SRM / EBC	
EFFICIENCY	
OG / FG	

INGREDIENTS

....	....	....	....
....	....	....	....
....	....	....	....
....	....	....	....
....	....	....	....

FERMENTATION

SAMPLE DATE	TEMPERATURE	GRAVITY

BREWING NOTES

TASTE

HOP NOTE	☆☆☆☆☆
YEAST NOTE	☆☆☆☆☆
AROMA	☆☆☆☆☆
FLAVOUR	☆☆☆☆☆

BEER NAME	IBU
STYLE	ABV
BATCH #	SRM / EBC
BATCH SIZE	EFFICIENCY
DATE	OG / FG

INGREDIENTS

FERMENTATION

SAMPLE DATE	TEMPERATURE	GRAVITY

BREWING NOTES

TASTE

HOP NOTE	☆☆☆☆☆
YEAST NOTE	☆☆☆☆☆
AROMA	☆☆☆☆☆
FLAVOUR	☆☆☆☆☆

- BEERNAME
- STYLE
- BATCH #
- BATCH SIZE
- DATE

- IBU
- ABV
- SRM / EBC
- EFFICIENCY
- OG / FG

INGREDIENTS

FERMENTATION

SAMPLE DATE	TEMPERATURE	GRAVITY

BREWING NOTES

TASTE

- HOP NOTE ☆☆☆☆☆
- YEAST NOTE ☆☆☆☆☆
- AROMA ☆☆☆☆☆
- FLAVOUR ☆☆☆☆☆

BEER NAME		IBU
STYLE		ABV
BATCH #		SRM / EBC
BATCH SIZE		EFFICIENCY
DATE		OG / FG

INGREDIENTS

FERMENTATION

SAMPLE DATE	TEMPERATURE	GRAVITY

BREWING NOTES

TASTE

HOP NOTE		☆☆☆☆☆
YEAST NOTE		☆☆☆☆☆
AROMA		☆☆☆☆☆
FLAVOUR		☆☆☆☆☆

BEERNAME	IBU
STYLE	ABV
BATCH #	SRM / EBC
BATCH SIZE	EFFICIENCY
DATE	OG / FG

INGREDIENTS

FERMENTATION

SAMPLE DATE	TEMPERATURE	GRAVITY

BREWING NOTES

TASTE

HOP NOTE	☆☆☆☆☆
YEAST NOTE	☆☆☆☆☆
AROMA	☆☆☆☆☆
FLAVOUR	☆☆☆☆☆

BEER NAME		IBU
STYLE		ABV
BATCH #		SRM / EBC
BATCH SIZE		EFFICIENCY
DATE		OG / FG

INGREDIENTS

FERMENTATION

SAMPLE DATE	TEMPERATURE	GRAVITY

BREWING NOTES

TASTE

HOP NOTE	☆☆☆☆☆
YEAST NOTE	☆☆☆☆☆
AROMA	☆☆☆☆☆
FLAVOUR	☆☆☆☆☆

BEER NAME		IBU
STYLE		ABV
BATCH #		SRM / EBC
BATCH SIZE		EFFICIENCY
DATE		OG / FG

INGREDIENTS

FERMENTATION

SAMPLE DATE	TEMPERATURE	GRAVITY

BREWING NOTES	TASTE	
	HOP NOTE	☆☆☆☆☆
	YEAST NOTE	☆☆☆☆☆
	AROMA	☆☆☆☆☆
	FLAVOUR	☆☆☆☆☆

BEER NAME		**IBU**	
STYLE		**ABV**	
BATCH #		**SRM / EBC**	
BATCH SIZE		**EFFICIENCY**	
DATE		**OG / FG**	

INGREDIENTS

....	....	....	....
....	....	....	....
....	....	....	....
....	....	....	....
....	....	....	....

FERMENTATION

SAMPLE DATE	TEMPERATURE	GRAVITY

BREWING NOTES

TASTE

HOP NOTE	☆☆☆☆☆
YEAST NOTE	☆☆☆☆☆
AROMA	☆☆☆☆☆
FLAVOUR	☆☆☆☆☆

BEERNAME		IBU
STYLE		ABV
BATCH #		SRM / EBC
BATCH SIZE		EFFICIENCY
DATE		OG / FG

INGREDIENTS

FERMENTATION

SAMPLE DATE	TEMPERATURE	GRAVITY

BREWING NOTES

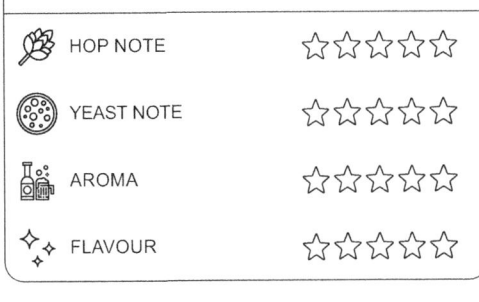

TASTE

	HOP NOTE	☆☆☆☆☆
	YEAST NOTE	☆☆☆☆☆
	AROMA	☆☆☆☆☆
	FLAVOUR	☆☆☆☆☆

BEER NAME		IBU
STYLE		ABV
BATCH #		SRM / EBC
BATCH SIZE		EFFICIENCY
DATE		OG / FG

INGREDIENTS

FERMENTATION

SAMPLE DATE	TEMPERATURE	GRAVITY

BREWING NOTES

TASTE

	HOP NOTE	☆☆☆☆☆
	YEAST NOTE	☆☆☆☆☆
	AROMA	☆☆☆☆☆
	FLAVOUR	☆☆☆☆☆

BEER NAME	
STYLE	
BATCH #	
BATCH SIZE	
DATE	

IBU	
ABV	
SRM / EBC	
EFFICIENCY	
OG / FG	

INGREDIENTS

FERMENTATION

SAMPLE DATE	TEMPERATURE	GRAVITY

BREWING NOTES

TASTE

HOP NOTE	☆☆☆☆☆
YEAST NOTE	☆☆☆☆☆
AROMA	☆☆☆☆☆
FLAVOUR	☆☆☆☆☆

BEER NAME		IBU
STYLE		ABV
BATCH #		SRM / EBC
BATCH SIZE		EFFICIENCY
DATE		OG / FG

INGREDIENTS

FERMENTATION

SAMPLE DATE	TEMPERATURE	GRAVITY

BREWING NOTES

TASTE

	HOP NOTE	☆☆☆☆☆
	YEAST NOTE	☆☆☆☆☆
	AROMA	☆☆☆☆☆
	FLAVOUR	☆☆☆☆☆

BEER NAME	IBU
STYLE	ABV
BATCH #	SRM / EBC
BATCH SIZE	EFFICIENCY
DATE	OG / FG

INGREDIENTS

FERMENTATION

SAMPLE DATE	TEMPERATURE	GRAVITY

BREWING NOTES

TASTE

HOP NOTE	☆☆☆☆☆
YEAST NOTE	☆☆☆☆☆
AROMA	☆☆☆☆☆
FLAVOUR	☆☆☆☆☆

BEER NAME		IBU	
STYLE		ABV	
BATCH #		SRM / EBC	
BATCH SIZE		EFFICIENCY	
DATE		OG / FG	

INGREDIENTS

....	....	....	....
....	....	....	....
....	....	....	....
....	....	....	....
....	....	....	....

FERMENTATION

SAMPLE DATE	TEMPERATURE	GRAVITY

BREWING NOTES

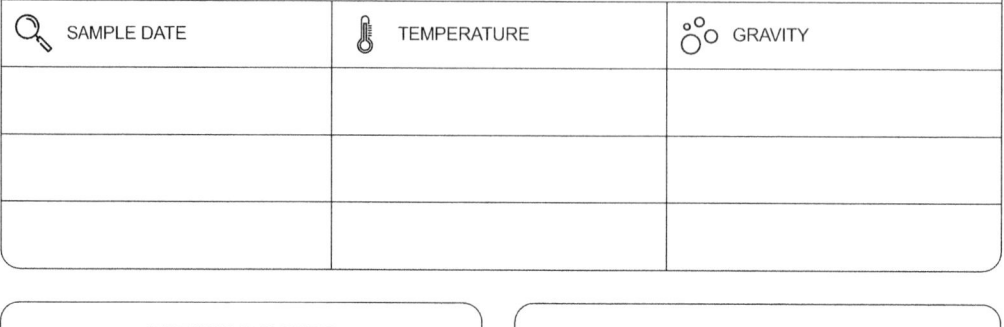

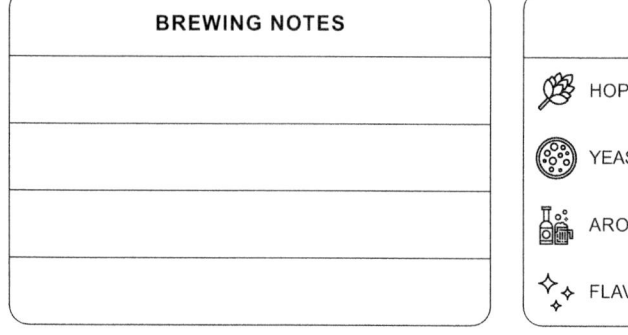

TASTE

HOP NOTE	☆☆☆☆☆
YEAST NOTE	☆☆☆☆☆
AROMA	☆☆☆☆☆
FLAVOUR	☆☆☆☆☆

BEERNAME	**IBU**
STYLE	**ABV**
BATCH #	**SRM / EBC**
BATCH SIZE	**EFFICIENCY**
DATE	**OG / FG**

INGREDIENTS

....	....
....	....
....	....
....	....
....	....

FERMENTATION

SAMPLE DATE	TEMPERATURE	GRAVITY

BREWING NOTES

TASTE

HOP NOTE	☆☆☆☆☆
YEAST NOTE	☆☆☆☆☆
AROMA	☆☆☆☆☆
FLAVOUR	☆☆☆☆☆

BEER NAME	IBU
STYLE	ABV
BATCH #	SRM / EBC
BATCH SIZE	EFFICIENCY
DATE	OG / FG

INGREDIENTS

....	....
....	....
....	....
....	....
....	....

FERMENTATION

SAMPLE DATE	TEMPERATURE	GRAVITY

BREWING NOTES

TASTE

HOP NOTE	☆☆☆☆☆
YEAST NOTE	☆☆☆☆☆
AROMA	☆☆☆☆☆
FLAVOUR	☆☆☆☆☆

BEER NAME	IBU
STYLE	ABV
BATCH #	SRM / EBC
BATCH SIZE	EFFICIENCY
DATE	OG / FG

INGREDIENTS

FERMENTATION

SAMPLE DATE	TEMPERATURE	GRAVITY

BREWING NOTES

TASTE

HOP NOTE	☆☆☆☆☆
YEAST NOTE	☆☆☆☆☆
AROMA	☆☆☆☆☆
FLAVOUR	☆☆☆☆☆

BEER NAME		IBU
STYLE		ABV
BATCH #		SRM / EBC
BATCH SIZE		EFFICIENCY
DATE		OG / FG

INGREDIENTS

FERMENTATION

SAMPLE DATE	TEMPERATURE	GRAVITY

BREWING NOTES

TASTE

HOP NOTE		☆☆☆☆☆
YEAST NOTE		☆☆☆☆☆
AROMA		☆☆☆☆☆
FLAVOUR		☆☆☆☆☆

BEER NAME		IBU
STYLE		ABV
BATCH #		SRM / EBC
BATCH SIZE		EFFICIENCY
DATE		OG / FG

INGREDIENTS

FERMENTATION

SAMPLE DATE	TEMPERATURE	GRAVITY

BREWING NOTES

TASTE

HOP NOTE	☆☆☆☆☆
YEAST NOTE	☆☆☆☆☆
AROMA	☆☆☆☆☆
FLAVOUR	☆☆☆☆☆

BEER NAME		IBU
STYLE		ABV
BATCH #		SRM / EBC
BATCH SIZE		EFFICIENCY
DATE		OG / FG

INGREDIENTS

....	....	....	....
....	....	....	....
....	....	....	....
....	....	....	....
....	....	....	....

FERMENTATION

SAMPLE DATE	TEMPERATURE	GRAVITY

BREWING NOTES

TASTE

	HOP NOTE	☆☆☆☆☆
	YEAST NOTE	☆☆☆☆☆
	AROMA	☆☆☆☆☆
	FLAVOUR	☆☆☆☆☆

BEERNAME	IBU
STYLE	ABV
BATCH #	SRM / EBC
BATCH SIZE	EFFICIENCY
DATE	OG / FG

INGREDIENTS

....	....	....	....
....	....	....	....
....	....	....	....
....	....	....	....
....	....	....	....

FERMENTATION

SAMPLE DATE	TEMPERATURE	GRAVITY

BREWING NOTES

TASTE

HOP NOTE	☆☆☆☆☆
YEAST NOTE	☆☆☆☆☆
AROMA	☆☆☆☆☆
FLAVOUR	☆☆☆☆☆

BEER NAME	IBU
STYLE	ABV
BATCH #	SRM / EBC
BATCH SIZE	EFFICIENCY
DATE	OG / FG

INGREDIENTS

FERMENTATION

SAMPLE DATE	TEMPERATURE	GRAVITY

BREWING NOTES

TASTE

HOP NOTE	☆☆☆☆☆
YEAST NOTE	☆☆☆☆☆
AROMA	☆☆☆☆☆
FLAVOUR	☆☆☆☆☆

BEERNAME		IBU	
STYLE		ABV	
BATCH #		SRM / EBC	
BATCH SIZE		EFFICIENCY	
DATE		OG / FG	

INGREDIENTS

FERMENTATION

SAMPLE DATE	TEMPERATURE	GRAVITY

BREWING NOTES

TASTE

HOP NOTE		☆☆☆☆☆
YEAST NOTE		☆☆☆☆☆
AROMA		☆☆☆☆☆
FLAVOUR		☆☆☆☆☆

🍺 BEER NAME	🌿 IBU
🌾 STYLE	🍾 ABV
🍻 BATCH #	🍺 SRM / EBC
🏭 BATCH SIZE	💲 EFFICIENCY
📅 DATE	🫧 OG / FG

INGREDIENTS

....	....
....	....
....	....
....	....
....	....

FERMENTATION

🔍 SAMPLE DATE	🌡 TEMPERATURE	🫧 GRAVITY

BREWING NOTES

TASTE

🌿	HOP NOTE	☆☆☆☆☆
🧫	YEAST NOTE	☆☆☆☆☆
🍶	AROMA	☆☆☆☆☆
✨	FLAVOUR	☆☆☆☆☆

BEER NAME	IBU
STYLE	ABV
BATCH #	SRM / EBC
BATCH SIZE	EFFICIENCY
DATE	OG / FG

INGREDIENTS

FERMENTATION

SAMPLE DATE	TEMPERATURE	GRAVITY

BREWING NOTES

TASTE

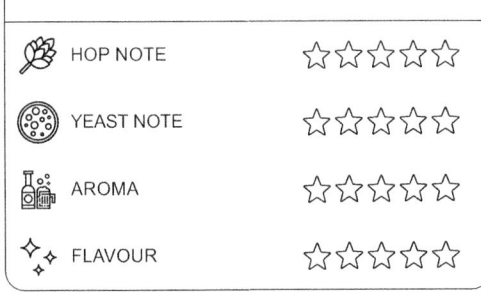

- HOP NOTE ☆☆☆☆☆
- YEAST NOTE ☆☆☆☆☆
- AROMA ☆☆☆☆☆
- FLAVOUR ☆☆☆☆☆

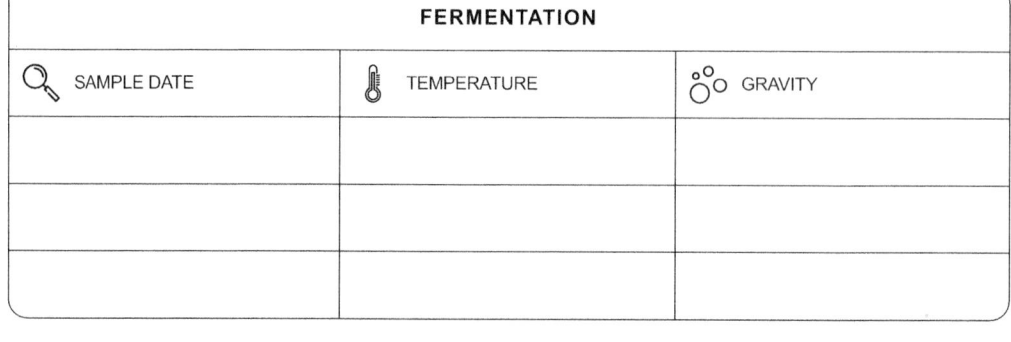

BEER NAME		IBU
STYLE		ABV
BATCH #		SRM / EBC
BATCH SIZE		EFFICIENCY
DATE		OG / FG

INGREDIENTS

....	....	....	....
....	....	....	....
....	....	....	....
....	....	....	....
....	....	....	....

FERMENTATION

SAMPLE DATE	TEMPERATURE	GRAVITY

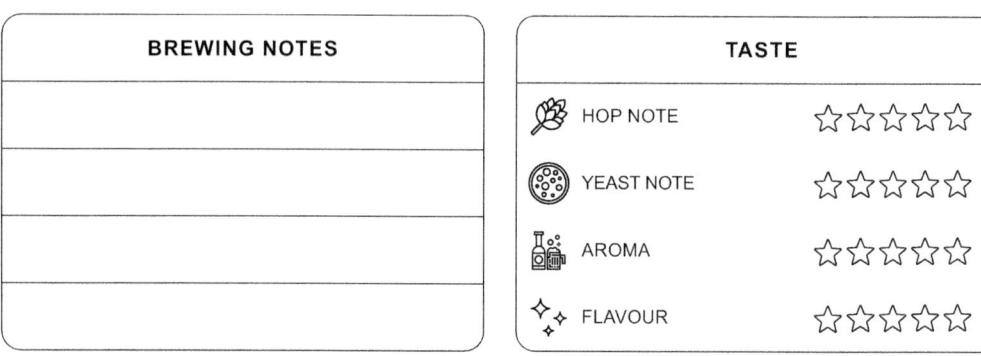

BREWING NOTES

TASTE

HOP NOTE		☆☆☆☆☆
YEAST NOTE		☆☆☆☆☆
AROMA		☆☆☆☆☆
FLAVOUR		☆☆☆☆☆

BEER NAME	IBU
STYLE	ABV
BATCH #	SRM / EBC
BATCH SIZE	EFFICIENCY
DATE	OG / FG

INGREDIENTS

FERMENTATION

SAMPLE DATE	TEMPERATURE	GRAVITY

BREWING NOTES

TASTE

HOP NOTE	☆☆☆☆☆
YEAST NOTE	☆☆☆☆☆
AROMA	☆☆☆☆☆
FLAVOUR	☆☆☆☆☆

BEER NAME		IBU	
STYLE		ABV	
BATCH #		SRM / EBC	
BATCH SIZE		EFFICIENCY	
DATE		OG / FG	

INGREDIENTS

....	....	....	....
....	....	....	....
....	....	....	....
....	....	....	....
....	....	....	....

FERMENTATION

SAMPLE DATE	TEMPERATURE	GRAVITY

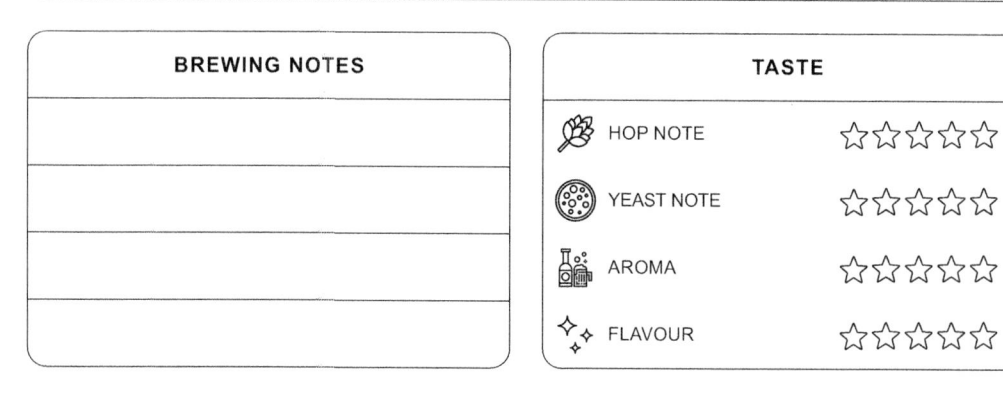

BREWING NOTES

TASTE

HOP NOTE	☆☆☆☆☆
YEAST NOTE	☆☆☆☆☆
AROMA	☆☆☆☆☆
FLAVOUR	☆☆☆☆☆

🍺 BEER NAME	🌿 IBU
🌾 STYLE	🍾 ABV
🍻 BATCH #	🍺 SRM / EBC
🏭 BATCH SIZE	⚙️ EFFICIENCY
📅 DATE	💧 OG / FG

INGREDIENTS

....	....	....	....
....	....	....	....
....	....	....	....
....	....	....	....
....	....	....	....

FERMENTATION

🔍 SAMPLE DATE	🌡️ TEMPERATURE	💧 GRAVITY

BREWING NOTES

TASTE

🌿 HOP NOTE	☆☆☆☆☆
🧫 YEAST NOTE	☆☆☆☆☆
🧪 AROMA	☆☆☆☆☆
✨ FLAVOUR	☆☆☆☆☆

🍺 BEERNAME	🌿 IBU
🌾 STYLE	🍾 ABV
🍻 BATCH #	🍺 SRM / EBC
🏭 BATCH SIZE	⚙️ EFFICIENCY
📅 DATE	⚗️ OG / FG

INGREDIENTS

....	....
....	....
....	....
....	....
....	....

FERMENTATION

🔍 SAMPLE DATE	🌡️ TEMPERATURE	⚗️ GRAVITY

BREWING NOTES

TASTE

🌿 HOP NOTE	☆☆☆☆☆
🧫 YEAST NOTE	☆☆☆☆☆
🍾 AROMA	☆☆☆☆☆
✨ FLAVOUR	☆☆☆☆☆

BEER NAME		IBU
STYLE		ABV
BATCH #		SRM / EBC
BATCH SIZE		EFFICIENCY
DATE		OG / FG

INGREDIENTS

FERMENTATION

SAMPLE DATE	TEMPERATURE	GRAVITY

BREWING NOTES

TASTE

HOP NOTE		☆☆☆☆☆
YEAST NOTE		☆☆☆☆☆
AROMA		☆☆☆☆☆
FLAVOUR		☆☆☆☆☆

BEER NAME		**IBU**	
STYLE		**ABV**	
BATCH #		**SRM / EBC**	
BATCH SIZE		**EFFICIENCY**	
DATE		**OG / FG**	

INGREDIENTS

....	....
....	....
....	....
....	....
....	....

FERMENTATION

SAMPLE DATE	TEMPERATURE	GRAVITY

BREWING NOTES

TASTE

HOP NOTE	☆☆☆☆☆
YEAST NOTE	☆☆☆☆☆
AROMA	☆☆☆☆☆
FLAVOUR	☆☆☆☆☆

BEERNAME	IBU
STYLE	ABV
BATCH #	SRM / EBC
BATCH SIZE	EFFICIENCY
DATE	OG / FG

INGREDIENTS

....	....
....	....
....	....
....	....
....	....

FERMENTATION

SAMPLE DATE	TEMPERATURE	GRAVITY

BREWING NOTES

TASTE

HOP NOTE	☆☆☆☆☆
YEAST NOTE	☆☆☆☆☆
AROMA	☆☆☆☆☆
FLAVOUR	☆☆☆☆☆

BEER NAME		IBU
STYLE		ABV
BATCH #		SRM / EBC
BATCH SIZE		EFFICIENCY
DATE		OG / FG

INGREDIENTS

FERMENTATION

SAMPLE DATE	TEMPERATURE	GRAVITY

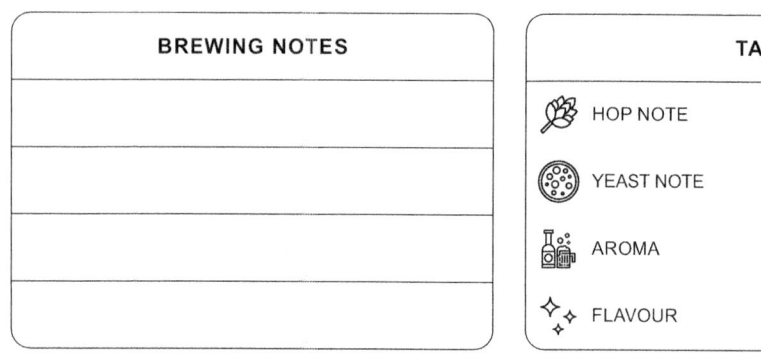

BREWING NOTES

TASTE

HOP NOTE	☆☆☆☆☆
YEAST NOTE	☆☆☆☆☆
AROMA	☆☆☆☆☆
FLAVOUR	☆☆☆☆☆

BEER NAME	
STYLE	
BATCH #	
BATCH SIZE	
DATE	

IBU	
ABV	
SRM / EBC	
EFFICIENCY	
OG / FG	

INGREDIENTS

FERMENTATION

SAMPLE DATE	TEMPERATURE	GRAVITY

BREWING NOTES

TASTE

HOP NOTE	☆☆☆☆☆
YEAST NOTE	☆☆☆☆☆
AROMA	☆☆☆☆☆
FLAVOUR	☆☆☆☆☆

BEER NAME		IBU	
STYLE		ABV	
BATCH #		SRM / EBC	
BATCH SIZE		EFFICIENCY	
DATE		OG / FG	

INGREDIENTS

FERMENTATION

SAMPLE DATE	TEMPERATURE	GRAVITY

BREWING NOTES

TASTE

HOP NOTE	☆☆☆☆☆
YEAST NOTE	☆☆☆☆☆
AROMA	☆☆☆☆☆
FLAVOUR	☆☆☆☆☆

BEER NAME		IBU
STYLE		ABV
BATCH #		SRM / EBC
BATCH SIZE		EFFICIENCY
DATE		OG / FG

INGREDIENTS

FERMENTATION

SAMPLE DATE	TEMPERATURE	GRAVITY

BREWING NOTES

TASTE

HOP NOTE ☆☆☆☆☆

YEAST NOTE ☆☆☆☆☆

AROMA ☆☆☆☆☆

FLAVOUR ☆☆☆☆☆

BEER NAME	IBU
STYLE	ABV
BATCH #	SRM / EBC
BATCH SIZE	EFFICIENCY
DATE	OG / FG

INGREDIENTS

FERMENTATION

SAMPLE DATE	TEMPERATURE	GRAVITY

BREWING NOTES

TASTE

HOP NOTE	☆☆☆☆☆
YEAST NOTE	☆☆☆☆☆
AROMA	☆☆☆☆☆
FLAVOUR	☆☆☆☆☆

BEERNAME		IBU	
STYLE		ABV	
BATCH #		SRM / EBC	
BATCH SIZE		EFFICIENCY	
DATE		OG / FG	

INGREDIENTS

....	....	....	....
....	....	....	....
....	....	....	....
....	....	....	....
....	....	....	....

FERMENTATION

SAMPLE DATE	TEMPERATURE	GRAVITY

BREWING NOTES

TASTE

HOP NOTE		☆☆☆☆☆
YEAST NOTE		☆☆☆☆☆
AROMA		☆☆☆☆☆
FLAVOUR		☆☆☆☆☆

BEER NAME		IBU
STYLE		ABV
BATCH #		SRM / EBC
BATCH SIZE		EFFICIENCY
DATE		OG / FG

INGREDIENTS

FERMENTATION

SAMPLE DATE	TEMPERATURE	GRAVITY

BREWING NOTES

TASTE

	HOP NOTE	☆☆☆☆☆
	YEAST NOTE	☆☆☆☆☆
	AROMA	☆☆☆☆☆
	FLAVOUR	☆☆☆☆☆

BEER NAME	
STYLE	
BATCH #	
BATCH SIZE	
DATE	

IBU	
ABV	
SRM / EBC	
EFFICIENCY	
OG / FG	

INGREDIENTS

FERMENTATION

SAMPLE DATE	TEMPERATURE	GRAVITY

BREWING NOTES

TASTE

HOP NOTE	☆☆☆☆☆
YEAST NOTE	☆☆☆☆☆
AROMA	☆☆☆☆☆
FLAVOUR	☆☆☆☆☆

BEER NAME		IBU	
STYLE		ABV	
BATCH #		SRM / EBC	
BATCH SIZE		EFFICIENCY	
DATE		OG / FG	

INGREDIENTS

FERMENTATION

SAMPLE DATE	TEMPERATURE	GRAVITY

BREWING NOTES

TASTE

HOP NOTE	☆☆☆☆☆
YEAST NOTE	☆☆☆☆☆
AROMA	☆☆☆☆☆
FLAVOUR	☆☆☆☆☆

BEER NAME	**IBU**
STYLE	**ABV**
BATCH #	**SRM / EBC**
BATCH SIZE	**EFFICIENCY**
DATE	**OG / FG**

INGREDIENTS

....	....	....	....
....	....	....	....
....	....	....	....
....	....	....	....
....	....	....	....

FERMENTATION

SAMPLE DATE	TEMPERATURE	GRAVITY

BREWING NOTES

TASTE

HOP NOTE	☆☆☆☆☆
YEAST NOTE	☆☆☆☆☆
AROMA	☆☆☆☆☆
FLAVOUR	☆☆☆☆☆

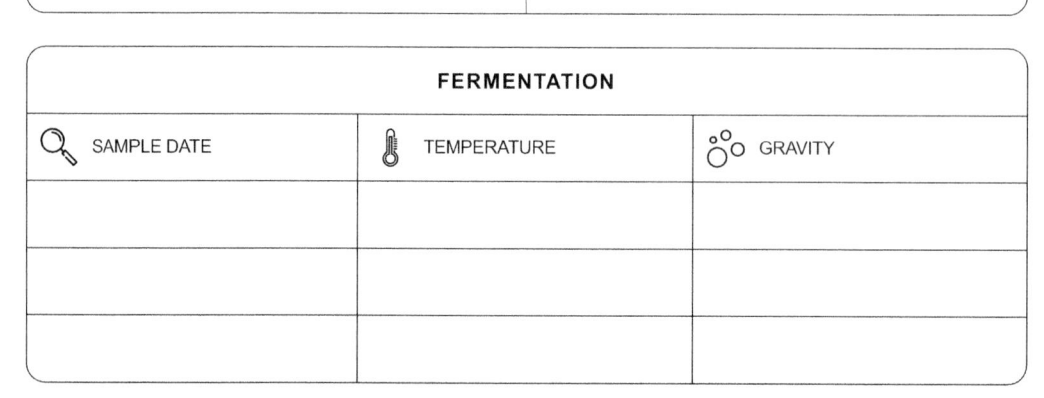

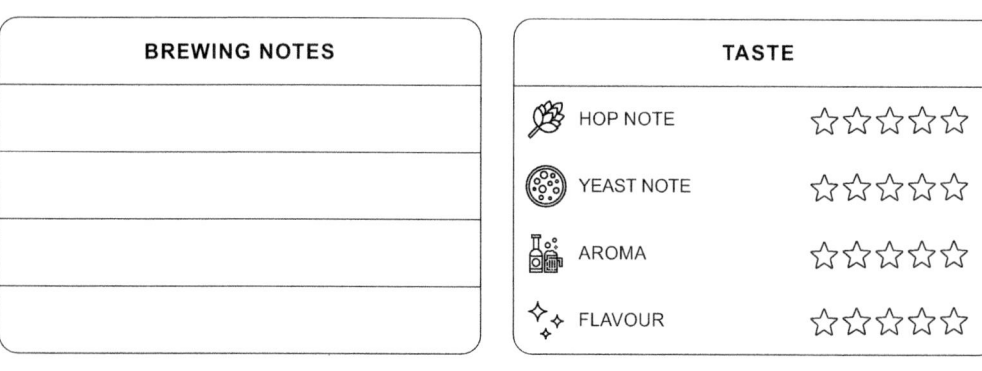

BEER NAME	
STYLE	
BATCH #	
BATCH SIZE	
DATE	

IBU	
ABV	
SRM / EBC	
EFFICIENCY	
OG / FG	

INGREDIENTS

FERMENTATION

SAMPLE DATE	TEMPERATURE	GRAVITY

BREWING NOTES

TASTE

HOP NOTE	☆☆☆☆☆
YEAST NOTE	☆☆☆☆☆
AROMA	☆☆☆☆☆
FLAVOUR	☆☆☆☆☆

BEERNAME		IBU	
STYLE		ABV	
BATCH #		SRM / EBC	
BATCH SIZE		EFFICIENCY	
DATE		OG / FG	

INGREDIENTS

FERMENTATION

SAMPLE DATE	TEMPERATURE	GRAVITY

BREWING NOTES

TASTE

HOP NOTE	☆☆☆☆☆
YEAST NOTE	☆☆☆☆☆
AROMA	☆☆☆☆☆
FLAVOUR	☆☆☆☆☆

BEER NAME	IBU
STYLE	ABV
BATCH #	SRM / EBC
BATCH SIZE	EFFICIENCY
DATE	OG / FG

INGREDIENTS

FERMENTATION

SAMPLE DATE	TEMPERATURE	GRAVITY

BREWING NOTES

TASTE

HOP NOTE	☆☆☆☆☆
YEAST NOTE	☆☆☆☆☆
AROMA	☆☆☆☆☆
FLAVOUR	☆☆☆☆☆

BEER NAME	IBU
STYLE	ABV
BATCH #	SRM / EBC
BATCH SIZE	EFFICIENCY
DATE	OG / FG

INGREDIENTS

FERMENTATION

SAMPLE DATE	TEMPERATURE	GRAVITY

BREWING NOTES

TASTE

HOP NOTE	☆☆☆☆☆
YEAST NOTE	☆☆☆☆☆
AROMA	☆☆☆☆☆
FLAVOUR	☆☆☆☆☆

BEER NAME		IBU	
STYLE		ABV	
BATCH #		SRM / EBC	
BATCH SIZE		EFFICIENCY	
DATE		OG / FG	

INGREDIENTS

FERMENTATION

SAMPLE DATE	TEMPERATURE	GRAVITY

BREWING NOTES

TASTE

HOP NOTE	☆☆☆☆☆
YEAST NOTE	☆☆☆☆☆
AROMA	☆☆☆☆☆
FLAVOUR	☆☆☆☆☆

BEER NAME		**IBU**	
STYLE		**ABV**	
BATCH #		**SRM / EBC**	
BATCH SIZE		**EFFICIENCY**	
DATE		**OG / FG**	

INGREDIENTS

....	....
....	....
....	....
....	....
....	....

FERMENTATION

SAMPLE DATE	TEMPERATURE	GRAVITY

BREWING NOTES

TASTE

HOP NOTE	☆☆☆☆☆
YEAST NOTE	☆☆☆☆☆
AROMA	☆☆☆☆☆
FLAVOUR	☆☆☆☆☆

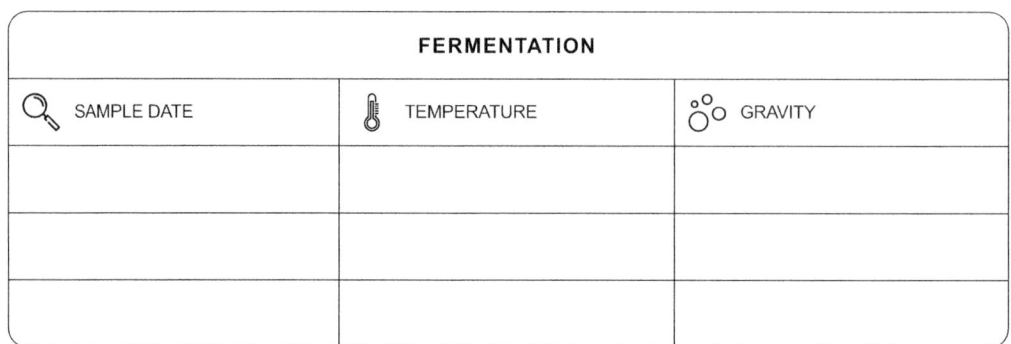

BEER NAME	IBU
STYLE	ABV
BATCH #	SRM / EBC
BATCH SIZE	EFFICIENCY
DATE	OG / FG

INGREDIENTS

FERMENTATION

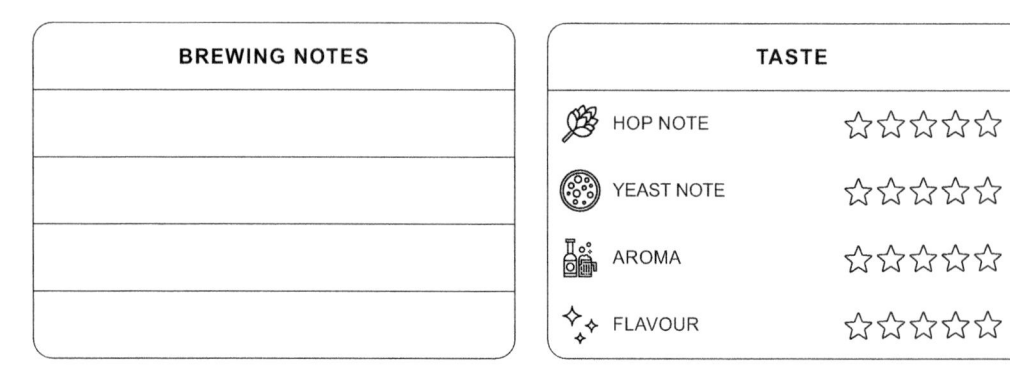

SAMPLE DATE	TEMPERATURE	GRAVITY

BREWING NOTES

TASTE

HOP NOTE	☆☆☆☆☆
YEAST NOTE	☆☆☆☆☆
AROMA	☆☆☆☆☆
FLAVOUR	☆☆☆☆☆

BEERNAME	
STYLE	
BATCH #	
BATCH SIZE	
DATE	

IBU	
ABV	
SRM / EBC	
EFFICIENCY	
OG / FG	

INGREDIENTS

FERMENTATION

SAMPLE DATE	TEMPERATURE	GRAVITY

BREWING NOTES

TASTE

HOP NOTE	☆☆☆☆☆
YEAST NOTE	☆☆☆☆☆
AROMA	☆☆☆☆☆
FLAVOUR	☆☆☆☆☆

BEER NAME		IBU
STYLE		ABV
BATCH #		SRM / EBC
BATCH SIZE		EFFICIENCY
DATE		OG / FG

INGREDIENTS

FERMENTATION

SAMPLE DATE	TEMPERATURE	GRAVITY

BREWING NOTES

TASTE

HOP NOTE		☆☆☆☆☆
YEAST NOTE		☆☆☆☆☆
AROMA		☆☆☆☆☆
FLAVOUR		☆☆☆☆☆

🍺 **BEER NAME**		🌿 **IBU**	
🌾 **STYLE**		🍾 **ABV**	
🍻 **BATCH #**		🍺 **SRM / EBC**	
🏭 **BATCH SIZE**		⚙️ **EFFICIENCY**	
📅 **DATE**		🫧 **OG / FG**	

INGREDIENTS

....	....	....	....
....	....	....	....
....	....	....	....
....	....	....	....
....	....	....	....

FERMENTATION

🔍 SAMPLE DATE	🌡️ TEMPERATURE	🫧 GRAVITY

BREWING NOTES

TASTE

🌿	HOP NOTE	☆☆☆☆☆
🧫	YEAST NOTE	☆☆☆☆☆
🍺	AROMA	☆☆☆☆☆
✨	FLAVOUR	☆☆☆☆☆

BEER NAME		IBU	
STYLE		ABV	
BATCH #		SRM / EBC	
BATCH SIZE		EFFICIENCY	
DATE		OG / FG	

INGREDIENTS

FERMENTATION

SAMPLE DATE	TEMPERATURE	GRAVITY

BREWING NOTES

TASTE

HOP NOTE	☆☆☆☆☆
YEAST NOTE	☆☆☆☆☆
AROMA	☆☆☆☆☆
FLAVOUR	☆☆☆☆☆

BEERNAME		IBU	
STYLE		ABV	
BATCH #		SRM / EBC	
BATCH SIZE		EFFICIENCY	
DATE		OG / FG	

INGREDIENTS

FERMENTATION

SAMPLE DATE	TEMPERATURE	GRAVITY

BREWING NOTES

TASTE

HOP NOTE		☆☆☆☆☆
YEAST NOTE		☆☆☆☆☆
AROMA		☆☆☆☆☆
FLAVOUR		☆☆☆☆☆

BEER NAME		IBU	
STYLE		ABV	
BATCH #		SRM / EBC	
BATCH SIZE		EFFICIENCY	
DATE		OG / FG	

INGREDIENTS

....	....	....	....
....	....	....	....
....	....	....	....
....	....	....	....
....	....	....	....

FERMENTATION

SAMPLE DATE	TEMPERATURE	GRAVITY

BREWING NOTES

TASTE

	HOP NOTE	☆☆☆☆☆
	YEAST NOTE	☆☆☆☆☆
	AROMA	☆☆☆☆☆
	FLAVOUR	☆☆☆☆☆

BEER NAME		IBU
STYLE		ABV
BATCH #		SRM / EBC
BATCH SIZE		EFFICIENCY
DATE		OG / FG

INGREDIENTS

FERMENTATION

SAMPLE DATE	TEMPERATURE	GRAVITY

BREWING NOTES

TASTE

	HOP NOTE	☆☆☆☆☆
	YEAST NOTE	☆☆☆☆☆
	AROMA	☆☆☆☆☆
	FLAVOUR	☆☆☆☆☆

BEER NAME	
STYLE	
BATCH #	
BATCH SIZE	
DATE	

IBU	
ABV	
SRM / EBC	
EFFICIENCY	
OG / FG	

INGREDIENTS

FERMENTATION

SAMPLE DATE	TEMPERATURE	GRAVITY

BREWING NOTES

TASTE

HOP NOTE	☆☆☆☆☆
YEAST NOTE	☆☆☆☆☆
AROMA	☆☆☆☆☆
FLAVOUR	☆☆☆☆☆

	BEERNAME
	STYLE
	BATCH #
	BATCH SIZE
	DATE

	IBU
	ABV
	SRM / EBC
	EFFICIENCY
	OG / FG

INGREDIENTS

FERMENTATION

SAMPLE DATE	TEMPERATURE	GRAVITY

BREWING NOTES

TASTE

HOP NOTE	☆☆☆☆☆
YEAST NOTE	☆☆☆☆☆
AROMA	☆☆☆☆☆
FLAVOUR	☆☆☆☆☆

BEERNAME		IBU
STYLE		ABV
BATCH #		SRM / EBC
BATCH SIZE		EFFICIENCY
DATE		OG / FG

INGREDIENTS

FERMENTATION

SAMPLE DATE	TEMPERATURE	GRAVITY

BREWING NOTES

TASTE

HOP NOTE	☆☆☆☆☆
YEAST NOTE	☆☆☆☆☆
AROMA	☆☆☆☆☆
FLAVOUR	☆☆☆☆☆

BEER NAME		IBU
STYLE		ABV
BATCH #		SRM / EBC
BATCH SIZE		EFFICIENCY
DATE		OG / FG

INGREDIENTS

FERMENTATION

SAMPLE DATE	TEMPERATURE	GRAVITY

BREWING NOTES

TASTE

- HOP NOTE ☆☆☆☆☆
- YEAST NOTE ☆☆☆☆☆
- AROMA ☆☆☆☆☆
- FLAVOUR ☆☆☆☆☆

BEER NAME		IBU	
STYLE		ABV	
BATCH #		SRM / EBC	
BATCH SIZE		EFFICIENCY	
DATE		OG / FG	

INGREDIENTS

FERMENTATION

SAMPLE DATE	TEMPERATURE	GRAVITY

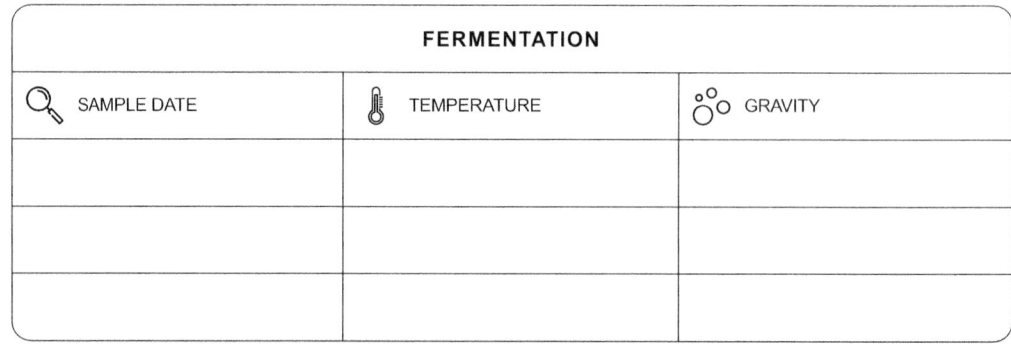

BREWING NOTES

TASTE

HOP NOTE	☆☆☆☆☆
YEAST NOTE	☆☆☆☆☆
AROMA	☆☆☆☆☆
FLAVOUR	☆☆☆☆☆

- BEER NAME
- STYLE
- BATCH #
- BATCH SIZE
- DATE

- IBU
- ABV
- SRM / EBC
- EFFICIENCY
- OG / FG

INGREDIENTS

FERMENTATION

SAMPLE DATE	TEMPERATURE	GRAVITY

BREWING NOTES

TASTE

- HOP NOTE ☆☆☆☆☆
- YEAST NOTE ☆☆☆☆☆
- AROMA ☆☆☆☆☆
- FLAVOUR ☆☆☆☆☆

- BEER NAME
- STYLE
- BATCH #
- BATCH SIZE
- DATE

- IBU
- ABV
- SRM / EBC
- EFFICIENCY
- OG / FG

INGREDIENTS

FERMENTATION

SAMPLE DATE	TEMPERATURE	GRAVITY

BREWING NOTES

TASTE

- HOP NOTE ☆☆☆☆☆
- YEAST NOTE ☆☆☆☆☆
- AROMA ☆☆☆☆☆
- FLAVOUR ☆☆☆☆☆

BEER NAME	IBU
STYLE	ABV
BATCH #	SRM / EBC
BATCH SIZE	EFFICIENCY
DATE	OG / FG

INGREDIENTS

FERMENTATION

SAMPLE DATE	TEMPERATURE	GRAVITY

BREWING NOTES

TASTE

HOP NOTE	☆☆☆☆☆
YEAST NOTE	☆☆☆☆☆
AROMA	☆☆☆☆☆
FLAVOUR	☆☆☆☆☆

BEER NAME		IBU	
STYLE		ABV	
BATCH #		SRM / EBC	
BATCH SIZE		EFFICIENCY	
DATE		OG / FG	

INGREDIENTS

FERMENTATION

SAMPLE DATE	TEMPERATURE	GRAVITY

BREWING NOTES

TASTE

HOP NOTE	☆☆☆☆☆
YEAST NOTE	☆☆☆☆☆
AROMA	☆☆☆☆☆
FLAVOUR	☆☆☆☆☆

BEERNAME	IBU
STYLE	ABV
BATCH #	SRM / EBC
BATCH SIZE	EFFICIENCY
DATE	OG / FG

INGREDIENTS

FERMENTATION

SAMPLE DATE	TEMPERATURE	GRAVITY

BREWING NOTES

TASTE

HOP NOTE	☆☆☆☆☆
YEAST NOTE	☆☆☆☆☆
AROMA	☆☆☆☆☆
FLAVOUR	☆☆☆☆☆

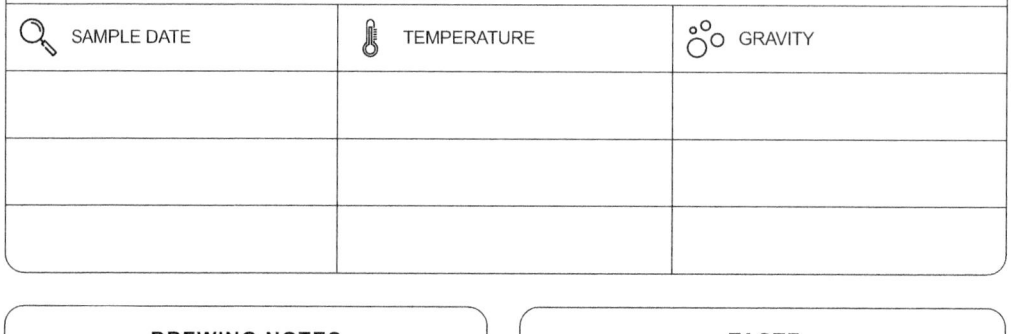

BEER NAME		IBU
STYLE		ABV
BATCH #		SRM / EBC
BATCH SIZE		EFFICIENCY
DATE		OG / FG

INGREDIENTS

FERMENTATION

SAMPLE DATE	TEMPERATURE	GRAVITY

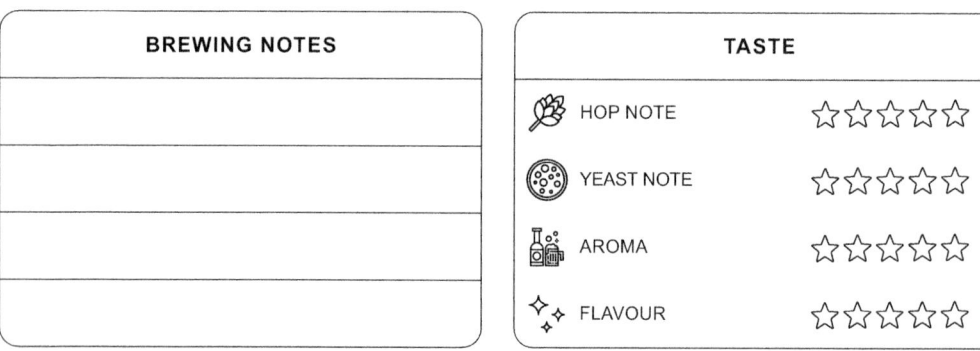

BREWING NOTES

TASTE

HOP NOTE	☆☆☆☆☆
YEAST NOTE	☆☆☆☆☆
AROMA	☆☆☆☆☆
FLAVOUR	☆☆☆☆☆

BEER NAME		IBU
STYLE		ABV
BATCH #		SRM / EBC
BATCH SIZE		EFFICIENCY
DATE		OG / FG

INGREDIENTS

FERMENTATION

SAMPLE DATE	TEMPERATURE	GRAVITY

BREWING NOTES

TASTE

HOP NOTE ☆☆☆☆☆

YEAST NOTE ☆☆☆☆☆

AROMA ☆☆☆☆☆

FLAVOUR ☆☆☆☆☆

BEER NAME	IBU
STYLE	ABV
BATCH #	SRM / EBC
BATCH SIZE	EFFICIENCY
DATE	OG / FG

INGREDIENTS

FERMENTATION

SAMPLE DATE	TEMPERATURE	GRAVITY

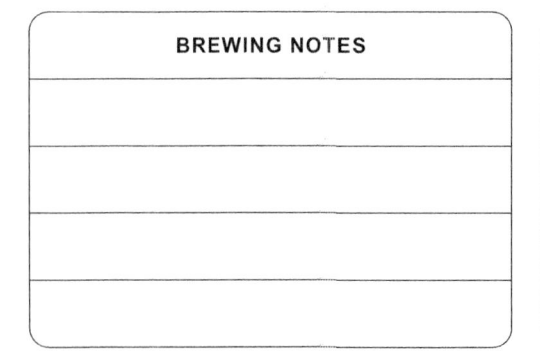

BREWING NOTES

TASTE

HOP NOTE	☆☆☆☆☆
YEAST NOTE	☆☆☆☆☆
AROMA	☆☆☆☆☆
FLAVOUR	☆☆☆☆☆

BEERNAME	
STYLE	
BATCH #	
BATCH SIZE	
DATE	

IBU	
ABV	
SRM / EBC	
EFFICIENCY	
OG / FG	

INGREDIENTS

FERMENTATION

SAMPLE DATE	TEMPERATURE	GRAVITY

BREWING NOTES

TASTE

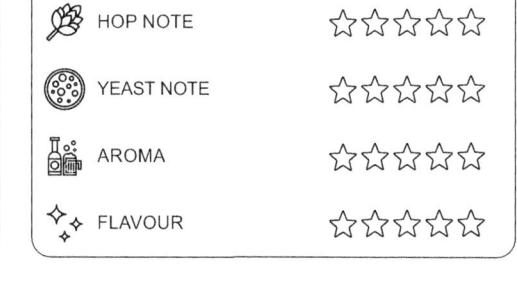

HOP NOTE	☆☆☆☆☆
YEAST NOTE	☆☆☆☆☆
AROMA	☆☆☆☆☆
FLAVOUR	☆☆☆☆☆

BEERNAME	IBU
STYLE	ABV
BATCH #	SRM / EBC
BATCH SIZE	EFFICIENCY
DATE	OG / FG

INGREDIENTS

FERMENTATION

SAMPLE DATE	TEMPERATURE	GRAVITY

BREWING NOTES

TASTE

HOP NOTE	☆☆☆☆☆
YEAST NOTE	☆☆☆☆☆
AROMA	☆☆☆☆☆
FLAVOUR	☆☆☆☆☆

BEER NAME	IBU
STYLE	ABV
BATCH #	SRM / EBC
BATCH SIZE	EFFICIENCY
DATE	OG / FG

INGREDIENTS

....	....	....	....
....	....	....	....
....	....	....	....
....	....	....	....
....	....	....	....

FERMENTATION

SAMPLE DATE	TEMPERATURE	GRAVITY

BREWING NOTES

TASTE

HOP NOTE	☆☆☆☆☆
YEAST NOTE	☆☆☆☆☆
AROMA	☆☆☆☆☆
FLAVOUR	☆☆☆☆☆

BEER NAME	IBU
STYLE	ABV
BATCH #	SRM / EBC
BATCH SIZE	EFFICIENCY
DATE	OG / FG

INGREDIENTS

....	....	....	....
....	....	....	....
....	....	....	....
....	....	....	....
....	....	....	....

FERMENTATION

SAMPLE DATE	TEMPERATURE	GRAVITY

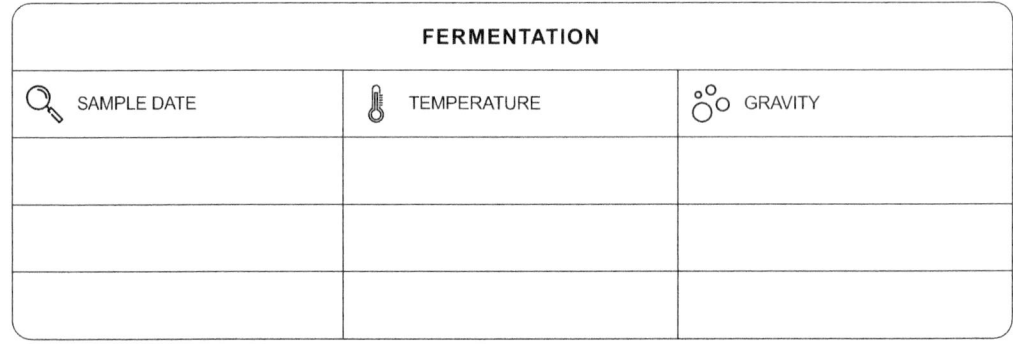

BREWING NOTES

TASTE

HOP NOTE	☆☆☆☆☆
YEAST NOTE	☆☆☆☆☆
AROMA	☆☆☆☆☆
FLAVOUR	☆☆☆☆☆

BEER NAME		IBU
STYLE		ABV
BATCH #		SRM / EBC
BATCH SIZE		EFFICIENCY
DATE		OG / FG

INGREDIENTS

FERMENTATION

SAMPLE DATE	TEMPERATURE	GRAVITY

BREWING NOTES

TASTE

HOP NOTE	☆☆☆☆☆
YEAST NOTE	☆☆☆☆☆
AROMA	☆☆☆☆☆
FLAVOUR	☆☆☆☆☆

BEER NAME		IBU
STYLE		ABV
BATCH #		SRM / EBC
BATCH SIZE		EFFICIENCY
DATE		OG / FG

INGREDIENTS

FERMENTATION

SAMPLE DATE	TEMPERATURE	GRAVITY

BREWING NOTES

TASTE

HOP NOTE	☆☆☆☆☆
YEAST NOTE	☆☆☆☆☆
AROMA	☆☆☆☆☆
FLAVOUR	☆☆☆☆☆

BEER NAME	
STYLE	
BATCH #	
BATCH SIZE	
DATE	

IBU	
ABV	
SRM / EBC	
EFFICIENCY	
OG / FG	

INGREDIENTS

FERMENTATION

SAMPLE DATE	TEMPERATURE	GRAVITY

BREWING NOTES

TASTE

HOP NOTE	☆☆☆☆☆
YEAST NOTE	☆☆☆☆☆
AROMA	☆☆☆☆☆
FLAVOUR	☆☆☆☆☆

BEERNAME		IBU
STYLE		ABV
BATCH #		SRM / EBC
BATCH SIZE		EFFICIENCY
DATE		OG / FG

INGREDIENTS

FERMENTATION

SAMPLE DATE	TEMPERATURE	GRAVITY

BREWING NOTES

TASTE

HOP NOTE		☆☆☆☆☆
YEAST NOTE		☆☆☆☆☆
AROMA		☆☆☆☆☆
FLAVOUR		☆☆☆☆☆

BEERNAME		IBU	
STYLE		ABV	
BATCH #		SRM / EBC	
BATCH SIZE		EFFICIENCY	
DATE		OG / FG	

INGREDIENTS

FERMENTATION

SAMPLE DATE	TEMPERATURE	GRAVITY

BREWING NOTES

TASTE

HOP NOTE	☆☆☆☆☆
YEAST NOTE	☆☆☆☆☆
AROMA	☆☆☆☆☆
FLAVOUR	☆☆☆☆☆

BEERNAME		IBU	
STYLE		ABV	
BATCH #		SRM / EBC	
BATCH SIZE		EFFICIENCY	
DATE		OG / FG	

INGREDIENTS

FERMENTATION

SAMPLE DATE	TEMPERATURE	GRAVITY

BREWING NOTES

TASTE

HOP NOTE		☆☆☆☆☆
YEAST NOTE		☆☆☆☆☆
AROMA		☆☆☆☆☆
FLAVOUR		☆☆☆☆☆

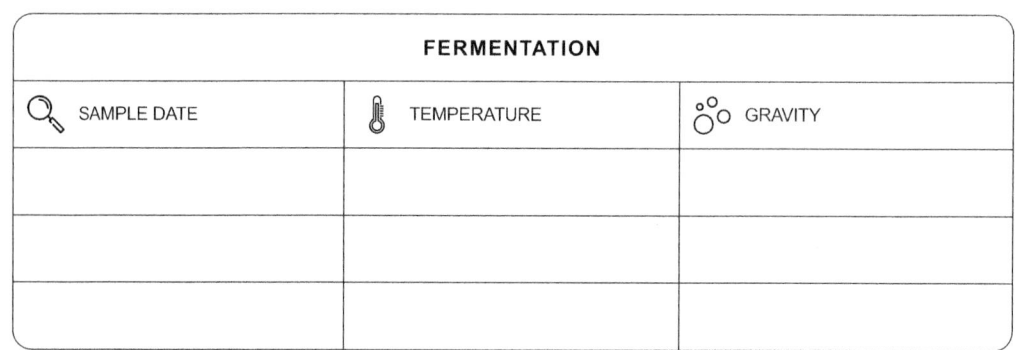

	BEER NAME		IBU
	STYLE		ABV
	BATCH #		SRM / EBC
	BATCH SIZE		EFFICIENCY
	DATE		OG / FG

INGREDIENTS

FERMENTATION

SAMPLE DATE	TEMPERATURE	GRAVITY

BREWING NOTES

TASTE

	HOP NOTE	☆☆☆☆☆
	YEAST NOTE	☆☆☆☆☆
	AROMA	☆☆☆☆☆
	FLAVOUR	☆☆☆☆☆

BEER NAME		IBU
STYLE		ABV
BATCH #		SRM / EBC
BATCH SIZE		EFFICIENCY
DATE		OG / FG

INGREDIENTS

FERMENTATION

SAMPLE DATE	TEMPERATURE	GRAVITY

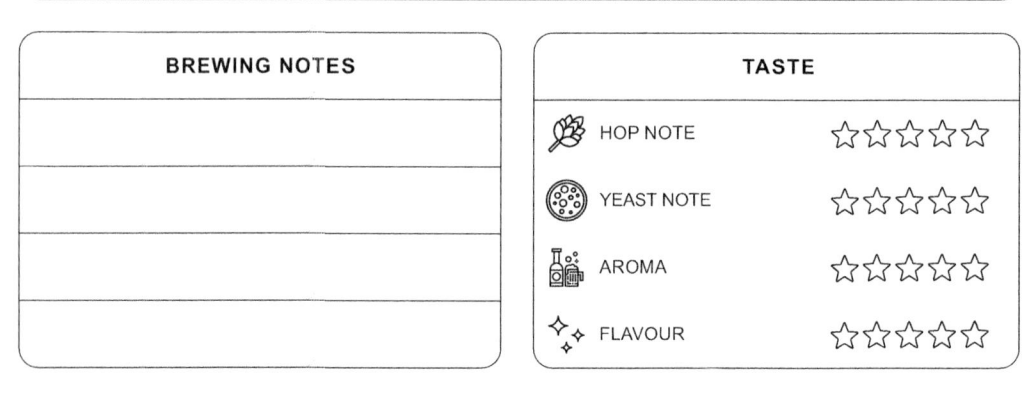

BREWING NOTES

TASTE

HOP NOTE	☆☆☆☆☆
YEAST NOTE	☆☆☆☆☆
AROMA	☆☆☆☆☆
FLAVOUR	☆☆☆☆☆

BEERNAME	IBU
STYLE	ABV
BATCH #	SRM / EBC
BATCH SIZE	EFFICIENCY
DATE	OG / FG

INGREDIENTS

FERMENTATION

SAMPLE DATE	TEMPERATURE	GRAVITY

BREWING NOTES

TASTE

HOP NOTE	☆☆☆☆☆
YEAST NOTE	☆☆☆☆☆
AROMA	☆☆☆☆☆
FLAVOUR	☆☆☆☆☆

BEERNAME	
STYLE	
BATCH #	
BATCH SIZE	
DATE	

IBU	
ABV	
SRM / EBC	
EFFICIENCY	
OG / FG	

INGREDIENTS

FERMENTATION

SAMPLE DATE	TEMPERATURE	GRAVITY

BREWING NOTES

TASTE

HOP NOTE	☆☆☆☆☆
YEAST NOTE	☆☆☆☆☆
AROMA	☆☆☆☆☆
FLAVOUR	☆☆☆☆☆

BEER NAME	**IBU**
STYLE	**ABV**
BATCH #	**SRM / EBC**
BATCH SIZE	**EFFICIENCY**
DATE	**OG / FG**

INGREDIENTS

FERMENTATION

SAMPLE DATE	TEMPERATURE	GRAVITY

BREWING NOTES

TASTE

HOP NOTE	☆☆☆☆☆
YEAST NOTE	☆☆☆☆☆
AROMA	☆☆☆☆☆
FLAVOUR	☆☆☆☆☆

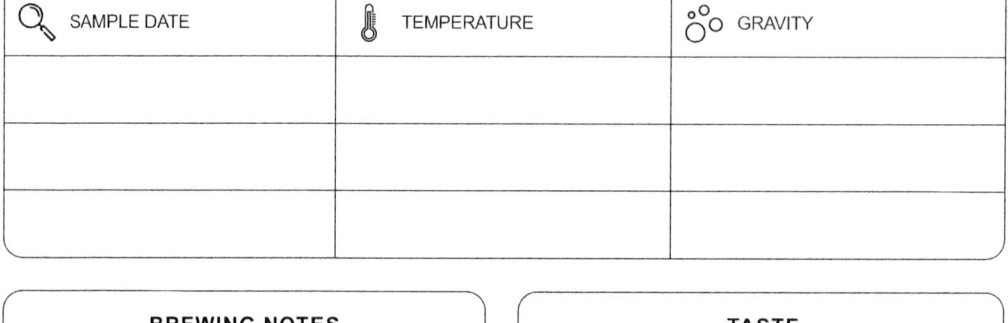

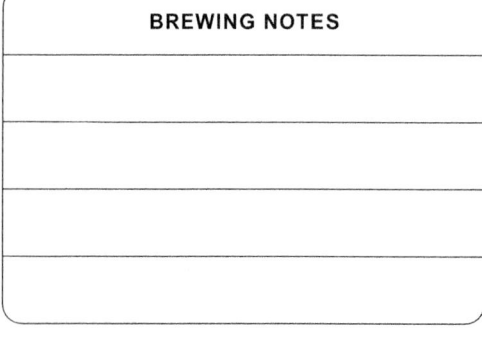

BEERNAME		IBU
STYLE		ABV
BATCH #		SRM / EBC
BATCH SIZE		EFFICIENCY
DATE		OG / FG

INGREDIENTS

FERMENTATION

SAMPLE DATE	TEMPERATURE	GRAVITY

BREWING NOTES

TASTE

HOP NOTE	☆☆☆☆☆
YEAST NOTE	☆☆☆☆☆
AROMA	☆☆☆☆☆
FLAVOUR	☆☆☆☆☆

BEERNAME	IBU
STYLE	ABV
BATCH #	SRM / EBC
BATCH SIZE	EFFICIENCY
DATE	OG / FG

INGREDIENTS

FERMENTATION

SAMPLE DATE	TEMPERATURE	GRAVITY

BREWING NOTES

TASTE

HOP NOTE	☆☆☆☆☆
YEAST NOTE	☆☆☆☆☆
AROMA	☆☆☆☆☆
FLAVOUR	☆☆☆☆☆

BEER NAME	IBU
STYLE	ABV
BATCH #	SRM / EBC
BATCH SIZE	EFFICIENCY
DATE	OG / FG

INGREDIENTS

FERMENTATION

SAMPLE DATE	TEMPERATURE	GRAVITY

BREWING NOTES

TASTE

HOP NOTE	☆☆☆☆☆
YEAST NOTE	☆☆☆☆☆
AROMA	☆☆☆☆☆
FLAVOUR	☆☆☆☆☆

BEERNAME		IBU	
STYLE		ABV	
BATCH #		SRM / EBC	
BATCH SIZE		EFFICIENCY	
DATE		OG / FG	

INGREDIENTS

FERMENTATION

SAMPLE DATE	TEMPERATURE	GRAVITY

BREWING NOTES

TASTE

HOP NOTE	☆☆☆☆☆
YEAST NOTE	☆☆☆☆☆
AROMA	☆☆☆☆☆
FLAVOUR	☆☆☆☆☆

BEER NAME	IBU
STYLE	ABV
BATCH #	SRM / EBC
BATCH SIZE	EFFICIENCY
DATE	OG / FG

INGREDIENTS

FERMENTATION

SAMPLE DATE	TEMPERATURE	GRAVITY

BREWING NOTES

TASTE

HOP NOTE	☆☆☆☆☆
YEAST NOTE	☆☆☆☆☆
AROMA	☆☆☆☆☆
FLAVOUR	☆☆☆☆☆

BEER NAME		IBU	
STYLE		ABV	
BATCH #		SRM / EBC	
BATCH SIZE		EFFICIENCY	
DATE		OG / FG	

INGREDIENTS

....	....
....	....
....	....
....	....
....	....

FERMENTATION

SAMPLE DATE	TEMPERATURE	GRAVITY

BREWING NOTES

TASTE

HOP NOTE	☆☆☆☆☆
YEAST NOTE	☆☆☆☆☆
AROMA	☆☆☆☆☆
FLAVOUR	☆☆☆☆☆

BEERNAME	IBU
STYLE	ABV
BATCH #	SRM / EBC
BATCH SIZE	EFFICIENCY
DATE	OG / FG

INGREDIENTS

FERMENTATION

SAMPLE DATE	TEMPERATURE	GRAVITY

BREWING NOTES

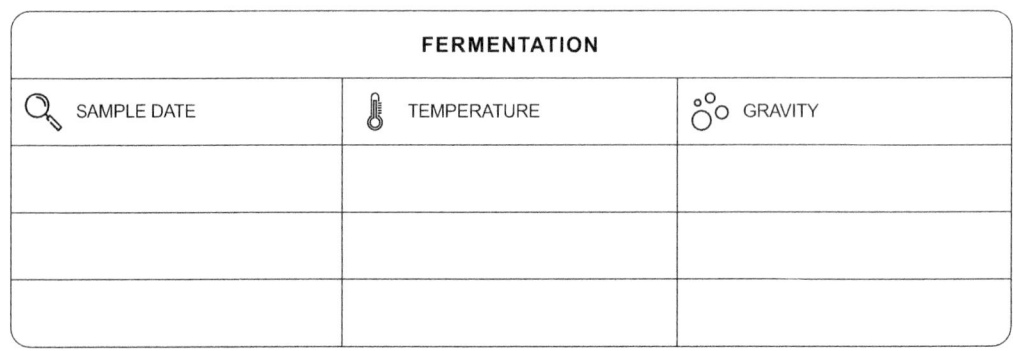

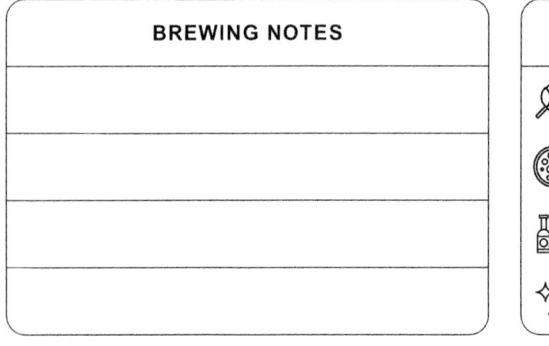

TASTE

HOP NOTE	☆☆☆☆☆
YEAST NOTE	☆☆☆☆☆
AROMA	☆☆☆☆☆
FLAVOUR	☆☆☆☆☆

BEERNAME		IBU
STYLE		ABV
BATCH #		SRM / EBC
BATCH SIZE		EFFICIENCY
DATE		OG / FG

INGREDIENTS

FERMENTATION

SAMPLE DATE	TEMPERATURE	GRAVITY

BREWING NOTES

TASTE

HOP NOTE	☆☆☆☆☆
YEAST NOTE	☆☆☆☆☆
AROMA	☆☆☆☆☆
FLAVOUR	☆☆☆☆☆

BEER NAME		IBU
STYLE		ABV
BATCH #		SRM / EBC
BATCH SIZE		EFFICIENCY
DATE		OG / FG

INGREDIENTS

FERMENTATION

SAMPLE DATE	TEMPERATURE	GRAVITY

BREWING NOTES

TASTE

HOP NOTE		☆☆☆☆☆
YEAST NOTE		☆☆☆☆☆
AROMA		☆☆☆☆☆
FLAVOUR		☆☆☆☆☆

	BEERNAME		IBU
	STYLE		ABV
	BATCH #		SRM / EBC
	BATCH SIZE		EFFICIENCY
	DATE		OG / FG

INGREDIENTS

FERMENTATION

SAMPLE DATE	TEMPERATURE	GRAVITY

BREWING NOTES

TASTE

	HOP NOTE	☆☆☆☆☆
	YEAST NOTE	☆☆☆☆☆
	AROMA	☆☆☆☆☆
	FLAVOUR	☆☆☆☆☆

BEERNAME	
STYLE	
BATCH #	
BATCH SIZE	
DATE	

IBU	
ABV	
SRM / EBC	
EFFICIENCY	
OG / FG	

INGREDIENTS

FERMENTATION

SAMPLE DATE	TEMPERATURE	GRAVITY

BREWING NOTES

TASTE

HOP NOTE	☆☆☆☆☆
YEAST NOTE	☆☆☆☆☆
AROMA	☆☆☆☆☆
FLAVOUR	☆☆☆☆☆

BEER NAME	IBU
STYLE	ABV
BATCH #	SRM / EBC
BATCH SIZE	EFFICIENCY
DATE	OG / FG

INGREDIENTS

FERMENTATION

SAMPLE DATE	TEMPERATURE	GRAVITY

BREWING NOTES

TASTE

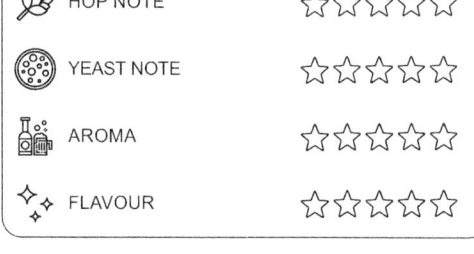

HOP NOTE	☆☆☆☆☆
YEAST NOTE	☆☆☆☆☆
AROMA	☆☆☆☆☆
FLAVOUR	☆☆☆☆☆

Copyright ©
All rights reserved. No part of this publication may be reproduced, distributed,
or transmitted in any form or by any means, including photocopying, recording,
or other electronic or mechanical methods, without the prior written permission
of the publisher, except in the case of brief quotations embodied in critical reviews
and certain other noncommercial uses permitted by copyright law.